BUT GOD SAID, "NOT SO!"

Tamara Bowman Wooden
But GOD SAID, "NOT SO!"
LIVING AGAINST MEDICAL SCIENCE

BUT GOD SAID, "NOT SO!"

LIVING AGAINST MEDICAL SCIENCE

TAMARA BOWMAN WOODEN

CONTENTS

Book Dedication

I would like to dedicate this book to several relatives who passed away fighting sickness and disease.

Ebony Kelly passed away at 41 years of age from lupus and seizures. She had kidney failure and was on dialysis. She experienced many episodes in the hospital in which she was near death but God brought her back. In September of 2016 Ebony completed her journey.

Thaddeus Kelly suffered from the same sickness, lupus, which manifested itself as seizures. At the young adult age of 21 Thaddeus had a seizure while waiting to be put on the list for a kidney. He didn't make it.

Acknowledgments

I would like to give all the glory to God for without Him I would not be here. The devil tried to steal my life numerous times but God said NO. It is in him I live and breathe and have my being. Praise God for his mighty acts in my life.

I want to give deep thanks and appreciation to my mother Gracie Bowman Holliday who continued to stand in the gap for me. She endured a lot trying to care for my brothers and having to make all those trips to the hospital with me. She continued to pray for my healing and I believe that is why God spared my life and I am here today.

My mother's best friend whom I have known all my life is Mother Annette Davison. Those two women were always together. They are the best of friends. Whenever I would get sick my mother would call for Mother Annette and they would take me to the hospital at the University of Michigan in Ann Arbor Michigan. Mother Annette, my godmother, would drive and they would both try to keep me alert. They are both retired nurses' aides. God had me in good hands.

My mother made a vow to the Lord. She told the Lord if He would deliver me she would serve Him for the rest of her life. As of today, she is still giving God all of her. I thank God for my mom, a true example for living a godly lifestyle. Now she lets me know that I'm on my own. She tells me to live my life for the Lord. He's brought me a long way.

Introduction

I was very young but I can remember having sick spells in which my head would hurt so badly until I would beg the adults to make it stop. I remember the saints praying for my healing. I was born into a godly family. My mother took me to church and everyone liked to hold me. I was her only girl and they were fond of me. They had not noticed the size of my head in proportion to my body. The doctor told my mother about my condition. The news was not good but my family went into prayer and asked all the saints to pray also. She put me in the late Papa Wells arms; that's when she made her vow to the Lord.

As my pastor often says I do not look like what I've been through. I was near death several times in my lifespan. Some hospital stays I cannot remember because I was in a comatose state so I had to rely on the narratives of others. I was very ill. I didn't know if I was going to make it but God said NOT SO. The devil cannot take my life unless God gives him permission and God told him NO.

In this book, I will share my testimony of how God has been very good to me. I am so grateful to God for His goodness and His mercy towards me. I give Him thanks.

Daybreak

On June 5, 1964 Gracie Bowman had a baby girl. Everyone thought I was a pretty little thing. No one noticed any problem until my mother noticed that when she would sit me up and prop me on pillows I would always fall over. As I began to throw up violently my mom and her best friend Mother Annette rushed me to the hospital. They thought that I was ill because I was always passed around to everyone at the church and maybe I had contracted something.

Doctors did many tests and decided that I was a hydrocephalic baby. We call it a water head baby. Fluid had collected in my brain and forced me to have. episodes of nausea and much swelling. I would throw up violently. It was a bitter bile and I felt horrible.

On one occasion, I had to stay at the hospital while my mother returned home to take care of my older brothers. They wouldn't feed me because they needed to take me into surgery so I would cry inconsolably because I was hungry. Finally, the nurses were told to give me something to eat. There was another baby in the hospital at the same time as me and that baby was suffering from hydrocephalus also. This baby, a Caucasian, passed away but I survived.

God spared my life. I was given a shunt, a system that was developed by a doctor in 1952 when he lost a child to this same condition. Before that time, children in my condition could not be helped; doctors just had to watch us die. There was no cure. God blessed a physician to develop a shunt to allow the fluid to drain off of the brain. I had the operation and went home and all seemed to be fine.

Mom was very cautious and careful with me She didn't want me playing rough so of course I loved to tussle and fight with my brothers. When I started school my mother made sure that the teacher knew of my medical condition so that she can be mindful of me and not let the other children hurt me. Actually, the students all protected me from harm. They wouldn't allow anyone to hurt me.

The Hydrcephalic Baby

Hydrocephalus is the buildup of fluid in the cavities (ventricles) deep within the brain. The excess fluid increases the size of the ventricles and puts pressure on the brain.

Cerebrospinal fluid normally flows through the ventricles and bathes the brain and spinal column. But the pressure of too much cerebrospinal fluid associated with hydrocephalus can damage brain tissues and cause a large spectrum of impairments in brain function. Although hydrocephalus can occur at any age, it's more common among infants and older adults.

Surgical treatment for hydrocephalus can restore and maintain normal cerebrospinal fluid levels in the brain. A variety of interventions are often required to manage symptoms or functional impairments resulting from hydrocephalus.

The signs and symptoms of hydrocephalus vary generally by age of onset. Common signs and symptoms of hydrocephalus in infants include changes in the head such as an unusually large head with rapid increase in size and a tense soft spot in the top of the head. Physical symptoms include vomiting, sleepiness. Irritability, poor feeding, seizures, eyes fixed downward (sunsetting of the eyes), and weakness in muscle tone and strength, touch and growth.

As they grow older they suffer headaches and blurred or double vision. They retain abnormally large heads, experience sleepiness, nausea or vomiting and unstable balance, poor coordination, poor appetite and seizures. They are irritable with changes in personality, problems with attention, decline in school performance and problems with walking and talking.

As a young adult, they will continue to experience headaches, difficulty in remaining awake or waking up, loss of coordination or balance, loss of bladder control or a frequent urge to urinate, impaired vision and decline in memory, concentration and other thinking skills that may affect job performance.

Among adults 60 years of age and older, the more common signs and symptoms of hydrocephalus are loss of bladder control or a frequent urge to urinate, memory loss, progressive loss of other thinking or reasoning skills, difficulty walking, often described as a shuffling gait or the feeling of the feet being stuck, poor coordination or balance and slower than normal movements in general.

The Shunt

The most common treatment for hydrocephalus is the surgical insertion of a drainage system, called a shunt. It consists of a long, flexible tube with a valve that keeps fluid from the brain flowing in the right direction and at the proper rate. One end of the tubing is usually placed in one of the brain's ventricles. The tubing is then tunneled under the skin to another part of the body where the excess cerebrospinal fluid can be more easily absorbed — such as the abdomen or a chamber in the heart.

People who have hydrocephalus usually need a shunt system for the rest of their lives, and regular monitoring is required.

There are other methods but this is the route that my doctor took for me.[1]

The information in this chapter was gathered from the original article : http:.//www.mayoclinic.org/diseases-conditions/hydrocephalus/basics/defini-tion/CON-20030706 with permission.

"If my people, which are called by my name, shall humble themselves, and pray, and seek my face and turn from their wicked ways; then will I hear from heaven, and will forgive their sin, and will heal their land." II Chronicles 7:14.

As I Grew Older

As I grew older and entered elementary school the shunt and tubing began to actually shorten as it grew out inside my body and I began to suffer the same symptoms again. Doctors discovered that the tubing that came from my brain to my stomach had shortened and fluid once again was collecting in my brain. I had to go into surgery again. Each time I had surgery I had to have my head shaved. The first time they only shaved the section that was needed and my mother combed over the rest. The next time she requested that they shave the whole head. I have beautiful long flowing hair and it grew back quickly. I was in the hospital for such a long time. I was seven years old and I remember going to school on the roof of the hospital.

Equipped with another shunt, this time the doctors put enough tubing so that as I grew the tubes lengthened. I went through high school. I have to admit I had to fight. I would fight boys or girls; it didn't matter to me. I was fearless. Not only had I outlived the doctor's prognosis but I even had two daughters. They were born with no complications and they had no lasting illnesses. They were and still are healthy.

My Children

When I was 19 years old I had my first daughter Kesha. When Kesha was three months old I had to have a fourth surgery. The next time I saw my baby she was six months old.

I was sick with my second daughter, Dameka. I lost so much weight until my bones seemed to stand out in my face. I had stones on my kidney. Dameka weighed only four pounds when she was born.

When my daughters, Keisha and Dameka, were small I once again had an episode and had to be hospitalized. This time I was totally unresponsive. Church members were called to rush to my aid and pray. I was rushed to the hospital where I remained in a comatose state. My condition was very grim. People came to my room and prayed for me. Once again the Lord breathed life into me and I was able to be released from the hospital.

I was very ill and my girls had to tend to me. They gave me my baths, combed my hair, fed me, and tried to take care of me. They said I was trying to give them directions and they couldn't understand what I was talking about. They were very sad about my condition. They had to miss extra curricula activities at school like sports and band because they had to come home and care for me in my illness. I suffered from confusion and did irrational things with no explanation and needed to be watched all the time. My daughters would cry because they did not understand and they didn't know what to do. Gradually the Lord allowed me to become whole again. Praise the Lord! The devil wanted to take me out but God said NOT SO.

Once Again

As I was walking on the sidewalk to my home I suddenly collapsed and fell on my face on the concrete. It was the shunt again. This time lupus had infected the shunt. I had to have emergency surgery. My mother was told that I wouldn't live overnight. When my pastor Elder Nathaniel Wells III came to visit, I asked him to dance for me because I was still alive. I was told he cried. I celebrate life again. God has brought me a very long way. It baffles the doctors. They did not expect me to live to reach adulthood and even so if I managed to live that long they expected me to have some degree of brain damage.

I have been an active member of my church and community. I have no mental issues; I am quite normal. Some would even describe me as exceptional. I love to cook; I was the leader of the women's group in my church for several years; I raised two girls and now I babysit my grands. God has truly been good to me whereof I am glad.

Lupus and Fibromaygia

As I began to age I developed more health issues. I had chronic pain in my joints and muscles and my lungs were affected. I went to California. The climate was really different there. My lungs ripped when I returned to Benton Harbor. I was diagnosed with lupus.

Lupus is a chronic disease where your body begins to fight itself (autoimmune disease). It causes damage to any part of the body such as your skin, joints and internal organs. This goes on for many years. The part of your body that fights off germs, bacteria and viruses (the immune system) goes haywire and does not protect your body by producing the antibodies that are needed to keep you from getting sick. In fact, your body starts to attack and destroy your healthy tissue. You begin to suffer from inflammation, pain and damage in different parts of your body. Even on good days you can have flare ups where you feel even worse and remissions where you actually feel that you are getting better. This is not a disease that you catch from others; but it can be hereditary. It can be life-threatening; I had to take chemotherapy. It can affect people of any age, sex, or race but it is two or three times more likely to develop with women of color between the ages of 15-44.

So, several of my relatives developed lupus also. This condition complicated my health issues even more. I was also told I had fibromyalgia which is a mild case of lupus thus the aching muscles and joints. Through it all I continued to press my way. In 2005 I had a hip replacement. I kept falling. The steroids for the lupus had eaten away at the hip bone. Lupus also attacked my brain.

The Angels Keep Watching Over Me

Of course, angels watch over us all the time but this time was very memorable. It was March of 2015 at about 3:30 am. I was sleeping in my apartment when one of my neighbors suffered a fire in her apartment. I was totally unaware of the situation until I woke up from a strange smell. I alarmed my grandson that we had to hurry out of the building. Since I was already suffering with my lungs, the smoke from the fire caused my lungs to bleed and I now walk around with a tank of oxygen. I had to move to another building but I'm still here! The devil is still defeated and I yet have the victory.

My Testimony As Told By Others

With a condition that affects the brain and has affected me since birth, there are many instances of which I would have no knowledge or recollection. This is my testimony as told by those who witnessed my condition as they would care for me.

My Mother, Gracie

The pregnancy went fine. Tammy was born without any complications. My only girl was beautiful. When Tammy was six months old I noticed that when she was sitting in a corner propped up on pillows she kept falling over. Then she started vomiting. The doctor measured her head and her head was the size of a one year old baby. I and my best friend Annette Davidson started the first of many trips to Ann Arbor to the University of Michigan.

When Tammy was six months of age, the doctor revealed that the vein that drains water from the brain didn't fully develop. As we were driving to Ann Arbor we had to constantly stop because Tammy kept throwing up something very bitter and foul. When we reached the hospital, I was told that Tammy needed surgery. "Did you notice the size of her head?" the doctor asked. I hadn't noticed. We brought her back home until the next time.

During the second surgery at three years of age they went in her head. They opened her skull and connected tubes to drain the fluid. They put a shunt in that drained all the way down to her stomach. Tammy was three years old. During the first surgery, she was a baby. While in the hospital Tammy threw up a lot. Mo

Addie Burton, our choir mother, insisted that the nurses get in there NOW. "You just going to sit there and let her die?" Tammy turned blue. They had to pump her stomach.

Tammy had to keep going back for checkups. A week later Tammy spiked a fever. The doctor told me that Tammy would not live, or if she lived she would be retarded, or that she would be crippled and not live past the age of ten. They also said she would not be able to have children. Mo. Addie wouldn't let anyone babysit Tammy but her.

On the third surgery Tammy was seven years old. They did testing all day. They drew fluid off her brain. This time we left her there. She stayed about seven days. I had to go home because I also have two boys. The next time I left the boys with my mother -in-law. Tammy did well for two to three years then she started vomiting again. She had outgrown her tubes. They appeared to have shortened as she grew. She was placed in a bubble and visitors had to dress in outfits and shoes to avoid germs. She stayed there a long time and attended school on top of the building.

For this surgery, they put tubes inside her body that would unwind as she grew. They seemed to be circular tubes. At age seven, her whole head was wrapped up.

Every time she had surgery after that they cut all her hair off instead of just one side. She grew back little curls.

Shunts were first made in 1952. The doctor who discovered it had a son in a motorcycle accident. When Tammy was in the hospital there were two of them with this water head problem. A Caucasian baby and Tammy. The Caucasian baby died. The doctors said there was nothing they could do for the babies before that discovery but let them die.

During the rides, Tammy, would throw up over everyone then fall into a deep sleep until we reached the hospital. The tubes had clogged up. Annette and I thought too many people were holding Tammy at church but that wasn't it. Everyone liked to hold Tammy and bounce her on their knee.

When school started, I was scared. I told the teacher about Tammy's condition so she could take precautions that kids wouldn't knock her down when playing. Kids started protecting her. She couldn't ride the bike. She had to sit on the porch. She was always messing with her brothers - Eric and Maurice. Tammy and Eric fought all the time during Headstart.

Tammy had her first daughter at age 19. Her name is Kesha. When Kesha was three months old Tammy had to have the fourth surgery. The next time she saw her baby Kesha was six months old. Her grandma said, "Can I keep her?" Tammy was bald on one side of her head. She used to comb it over. Her hair grew fast.

At age 19 Tammy cried because the nurses wouldn't feed her because she had to have surgery.   Nurses were fired because they didn't know what to do for her pain. Dr. Hopkins talked to Mercy Hospital and they were all fired.   Dr. Hopkins was very good. The shunt had corroded.

Tammy was sick with her second daughter Dameka. She lost so much weight, her bones seemed to stand out in her face. She had stones on her kidney. The baby weighed only four pounds.

When the kids had grown, Lisa Ervin found that Tammy was ill one day. Lisa said there was a spirit of death in the house.

"Withhold not correction from child: for
if thou beatest him with the rod, he
shall not die. Thou shalt beat him with
the rod, and shalt deliver his soul from
hell. My son, if thine heart be wise, my
heart shall rejoice, even mine."
Proverbs 23: 13, 14, 15.

Tammy developed lupus and the shunt tube had to be cut. I was told Tammy wouldn't live overnight. Tammy lost weight; she wouldn't eat. She appeared to be possessed. I took Tammy to my house. Lupus got into the shunt and went to the brain and she shut down.

Tammy had a hip replacement in 2005. She kept falling. Steroids for the lupus had eaten away at the hip bone. The doctor was godly. This was hip surgery. His name is Dr. Yergler. He said she would feel no pain. Tammy's girls would give her baths. They would say, "I'll lotion you but I'm not lotioning your tush." Her daughter Dameka had to stop sports to take care of her mother. Tammy had to wear Depends because she couldn't go to the bathroom by herself.

During the fifth surgery, the shunt broke in Tammy's stomach. On this occasion when Tammy was walking into my house she fell back and bumped her head on the ground. The shunt had broken and she was throwing up stuff. In the hospital Tammy felt that the nurses wouldn't change her bed. She yelled "Jesus" at every pain.

In March 2015 when Tammy's apartment complex caught fire; smoke got in her lungs and they started bleeding. Rayquon, her grandson, stayed with her and they had to get out at 3:30 a.m. A young lady in another apartment was cooking and grease on the stove started the fire.

When Tammy was young she got a whipping for going to the candy store (Mo Doss's house) across from the church. Tammy was not supposed to go across the street. I also beat Tammy with a wooden snow scraper for skipping school. I never gave Tammy a beating that she didn't deserve.

Mother Annette Davidson

Gracie (Sis) and I rode the highway a lot together taking Tammy to the hospital. I remember one night driving through the rain with no windshield wipers. It was raining very hard and I couldn't see but we kept going. Then the engine went out. I wasn't supposed to drive the car but Tammy had gotten sick so we went. In Kalamazoo, the sun came out. My dad was a mechanic so when we reached Benton Harbor he fixed the problem. Sis and I have been friends a long time.

My Aunt Lyneva Dalton

Tamara "Tammy" Maria Bowman Wooden by Aunt Lyneva Dalton

I remember when my sister called from the hospital on Friday, June 5, 1964 to tell momma and daddy that she had delivered a baby girl. Daddy asked, "What's her name" and Gracie said, "Tamara Maria Bowman". Of course daddy said "Ta what" because he was known to mess up difficult names to pronounce. Tammy, as we fondly started calling her was a pretty little yellow baby with a head full of hair. She looked so normal.

I remember at 5 months old Tammy was diagnosed as a Hydrocephalic (water head) baby. Tammy's head became larger than normal for a five-month-old baby. Although we cannot choose our families, God knew He had purpose for Tammy in her Mother's womb and she was born into a praying, faith holding, and miracle working family. Her family and the saints began to pray.

Tammy was referred to the University of Michigan Hospital. Many trips were made down I-94 eastbound carrying her to see Specialists. Tammy was diagnosed with this degenerating condition which usually leaves children crippled, physically deformed, blind and many more ailments.

However, Tammy didn't show any of those symptoms; the only signs she had was an oversized head and she cried a lot because of her headaches.

Her Grandma Letha and Grandpa loved them some Tammy, as we all did. They were a support system for Gracie as she had the other children, Maurice and Eric.

University of Michigan Hospital performed several surgeries on Tammy replacing the shunt to relieve the fluid pressure off her brain. I remember going to the University Hospital as a kid (not realizing how sick my precious niece was) and hearing the grown-ups asking how to navigate around the hospital and hospital staff saying follow the yellow lines and that would take us to where we needed to go. Gracie would spend countless days and nights at the hospital with Tammy. There was nothing too hard or out of the way for her to make sure her baby girl would pull through crisis after crisis.

The doctors told us that with this condition, Tammy's life expectancy was age ten and she would not be able to function as normal children would. As Tammy would physically grow, the shunt had to be replaced to accommodate her size. We knew when the shunt was messing up and causing distress because Tammy would start having severe headaches. I remember one time she was on her knees crying holding on to Grandma Letha asking her to please make it stop (those headaches). We then knew it was time for another trip to Ann Arbor to the hospital.

The University of Michigan Hospital doctors were amazed at how Tammy was progressing with the condition and coping in life. They called Tammy their "Miracle Baby". Tammy, by the Grace of God, lived past their life expectancy and has lived a normal life. Since she lived past what the medical studies indicated, the doctors were amazed. The doctors then said, we will watch her carefully because when she becomes a teenager or reaches puberty she will develop new problems and issues. God said it is not so, she shall not die but live to declare My works. The doctors then said she would never be able to have children. Well God said not so and she had not one but two beautiful healthy daughters.

Down through the years Tammy has had the enemy attack her body but nothing medically that any person could have experienced.

My Aunt (Ebony's mom)

I named Tammy "Tweety Bird" like the cartoon of the bird with the huge head. I was one of her babysitters.

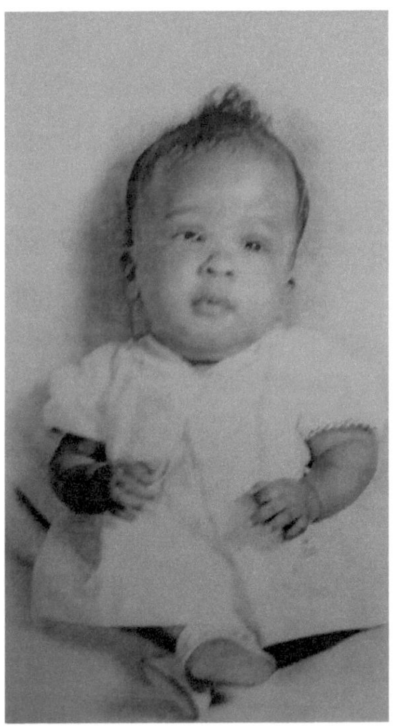

My Daughter Keisha Crenshaw

I am Tammy's oldest daughter. I am 33 years old. When I was in sixth grade my mother, Tammy, started to get sick. I was 12 or 13 years old. Tammy had to have her brain drained. She was slowly going into a baby stage. It was the lupus. I couldn't understand what my mother was saying. Tammy fussed. She kept trying to tell me something but it made no sense. Then she had to return to the hospital. She wasn't responding at all; she didn't recognize her children. She couldn't walk by herself.

When I had just graduated, Tammy caught pneumonia and her lungs got scarred. She lost a lot of weight. She was back in the hospital and unresponsive. She slipped into a comma. They weren't expecting her to live. She got headaches. Travon, her second grandson, was just born. It was 2008.

My sister Meka was bad from the time she was a baby. I didn't get bad until I was a teenager. Tammy said we got whippings and turned out alright.

When I was in sixth grade and Meka was in fourth, we girls had to feed Tammy, comb her hair, and bathe her. She wouldn't recognize or remember us and we would cry.

Tammy used to love to fight. She would fight men and women. Tammy is 52 years old. She is 19 years older than I am. Tammy went to California. The climate was really different there.   Her lungs ripped when she returned to Benton Harbor.

My Pastor Nathaniel Wells III

I believe this is an outstanding thing – Tammy is a living breathing testimony. Knowing her challenges, growing up as children together, she has quite a testimony. She has a close-knit family. Our families were close. She and my sister PJ were like best friends growing up. She was like a sister to me. We watched her progression growing up, her challenges, she's just a miracle that she's here. She was not supposed to be alive. We grew up with Tammy as children. We know about the things she battled physically. Most people could have gone down a dark tunnel of depression and walked aimlessly through life but knowing those challenges and how God brought her through is a miracle. She's not supposed to be alive. Those of us who know God know it is Him that has kept her and spared her life. He has a plan for her life. The Lord healed those scars. She has a testimony. He is not through with her yet.

My Friend Lisa Davis

The day it happened with us – me and Tyra – when they found her she wasn't really talking. When she went to the hospital she couldn't speak or talk. It was like she was comatose. They were praying; thy really didn't know if she would pull out of it or not.

God worked a miracle and she started pulling out of it. She lost all of her hair. She started speaking. I didn't understand the condition – the shunt in the brain. When this happened, she was an adult with kids. Tammy was friends with my aunt; I met her at church. The day she got really bad off sick they knocked on my door and said come pray for her. She was very sick. She ended up in critical care. She was like comatose for a while. They started her on treatments because she lost all of her hair. She basically had no life in her. God did a miracle and raised her up.

Seeing her up now, her beautiful hair, her moving around today – she couldn't walk or talk but God wasn't through with her yet. I would sit with her, hold her hand, and pray with her. It was amazing to see the transformation to see her transition and come out of it and God blessed her. Tammy's kids were teens. Meka was 15 or 16 years old, it must have been maybe fifteen years ago.

Reflections

By Jenise Blue

I was sitting in Community Church of God in Christ and I saw God's healing on Tammy's life many times but February 2017 I was led to sit by Tammy. At times I prayed for her; other times she commented and proceeded to tell me of her grandson Rayquan. We would laugh. She met my newly born grand daughter. I remember her smiling saying her grands would give her strength, and if you are not careful and let them pull on you, that they will take some of your strength too. We would share remarks of how she prayed and wanted the best for all of them. She would be smiling even them.

One Sunday God told me that Tammy would obey him. He told me how she had to say and do that which He, the Lord, gave her. In the mind He gave it to her how no one could do Tammy! He revealed her to be a chosen child, a chosen vessel of God, how no one could do Tammy and how it had been predestined, the life she had, good or bad.

It was revealed to me how the doctors didn't know how she was here, to their amazement, and how they tried medicines and procedures. God said that the doctors knew it was not them. Even when the doctors had given up, they somehow knew it was prayers and nothing but God! Then God said all the prayer in church went up teaching the doctors that the prayers of those praying people (the saints) work. God taught that they should have faith, and believe the works of the Holy Spirit. God answered a mother's cry. God then said, "I called her. I called her to do my will, my perfect will! Not man's, not mom's, not dad's, or brother's. But I am the Lord. For she is mine," said the Lord, "for my purposes."

As I would sit near Tammy, GOD gave me divinely inspired scriptures which you will find at the beginning of various chapters. Reverential fear came upon me and I am so blessed to be able to contribute to this anointed work.

Holding On For Life

In this phase of my book, I want to share with you some of the home conditions that we lived through. Not only was there a challenge with my health but our environment was very challenging as well.

"The righteous cry, and the LORD heareth, and delivereth them out of all their troubles. The LORD is nigh unto them that are of a broken heart; and saveth such as be of a contrite spirit." Psalms 34:17,18.

My Dear Mother

A virtuous woman is what I see when I look at my mother. My mom grew up in a Godfearing household, also known as a parent fearing household, where the children were taught to be obedient. Gracie's parents were both Holy Ghost filled. Gracie's parents taught her and her siblings to be responsible, loving, caring, honest, and hardworking individuals. Gracie was taught to be obedient to authority. Gracie and her siblings lost their mom at an early age. Gracie was about nine or ten years of age at the time. Her mom, Laura Yarbrough, died due to kidney failure but to God be the glory, Gracie's mom made arrangements just in case something should ever happen that her children would be taken care of. Isn't it something when you know your Lord and Savior Jesus Christ? He prepares you.

When Laura Yarbrough was called to glory the late Bishop Nathaniel Wells Sr. better known as Papa Wells and the late Mother Mildred Wells stepped in and watched over Gracie and her sister Betty. Gracie's father couldn't attend to her and her sister. The reason was they were girls and we know girls have to have special attention. Thank God for the late Mother Mildred Wells. So, Gracie's life went on, she became a teenager who lived a normal life.

Now from what I hear Gracie had it going on meaning she was a good-looking teenager. You know as a teenager we seem to forget about some of our teaching; I know I did. Our brains go in a different direction; things go haywire and we seem to lose control. Gracie had some good times, some bad times, and some funny times. She did her thing but she was well disciplined. She never did get in trouble with the law. She looks at me (her daughter) wondering what's wrong with that crazy girl, not remembering you reap what you sow, but worse. My mom made a comment once. She said she wished she could turn me into a boy. God gave her what she asked for which was me. Actually, I feel that my past actions can be compared with hers when she was young; it's the same things that she did, just in a different era.

42

"And we know that all things work together for good to them that love God, to them who are the called according to his purpose. For whom he did foreknow, he also did predestinate to be conformed the image of his Son, that he might be the firstborn among many brethren." Romans 8:28,29.

Our Home Life

Gracie was the oldest daughter in the Yarbrough family, but she was not the oldest out of her siblings. As time went by, her dad, Mosby, met a lady named Letha Gates and Mosby and Letha married. The Lord blessed my mom and siblings with another Holy Ghost filled mother. My grandma Letha stepped in and taught my mom and her sister Betty how to become good wives and mothers. They were even taught how to change diapers, wash diapers, and to become good homemakers. Gracie knew one day she would have a family of her own. She had enough practice to begin her journey as a wife and mother.

"Therefore thou art inexcusable, O man, whosoever thou art that judgest: for wherein thou judgest another, thou condemnest thyself; for thou that judgest doest the same things. But we are sure that the judgment of God is according to truth against them which commit such things. And thinkest thou this, O man, that judgest them which do such things, and doest the same, that thou shalt escape the judgment of God? Or despisest thou the riches of his goodness and forbearance and longsuffering, not knowing that the goodness of God leadeth thee to repentance? But after thy hardness and impenitent heart treasurest up unto thyself wrath against the day of wrath and revelation of the righteous judgment of God; Who will render to every man according to his deeds." Romans 2:1-6.

Dysfunction

Gracie married at the age of nineteen to a man named Eddie T. Bowman, who was, of course, my dad. Now my dad grew up as a hardworking man who also was a fighter. He was taught to fight when and if he had to; he was a boxer.

Gracie became a mother right away. Eddie, my dad, was taught about God and he was made to go to church by his parents, but he didn't know about holiness. In other words, he didn't have a relationship with God. Gracie bore her first child, Maurice. Maurice grew to love sports. Two years later Gracie bore another child; his name was Eric. Eric grew up to love music. Then two years later Gracie bore another child who grew up to cry all the time and that's Tammy. Not knowing Tammy was a very sick baby, my mom had to suffer many trials and tribulations.

My mom was beaten during her pregnancies - all three times. God knew Gracie could handle such a task covering her three children. God said He wouldn't put more on us than we could handle. As to Gracie's third child; God had a special calling on her life. Jeremiah 1:5 reads as follows. "Before I formed thee in the belly, I knew thee and before thou comest out of the womb I sanctified thee." Now the devil was waiting right at the door, but God gave Gracie a strategy for her and her daughter's life. God gave Gracie her little girl and Gracie gave her back to God for a covering. Gracie vowed to the Lord. She told the Lord if He would deliver her baby she would serve Him for the rest of her life. My mother was so faithful in her marriage; my aunt told me Gracie was the best sister-in-law in the world. That let me know my mom loved her in-laws. She would even make sacrifices for them. They would say Gracie is going to always be my sister-in-law.

Now as for my brothers and me, we grew up and we would try to protect our mom, but my dad had us so fearful of him. After seeing so much abuse I swore when I grew up I would never let a man beat me, that I would kill him. Thanks be to God it never happened. Now don't get me wrong, I had to do some fighting which was a little crazy. But no one died; thank you Jesus. I thank God my brothers were the opposite of my dad. My brother Eric never married. My brother Maurice treasures his wife; what a wonderful relationship that is. My brothers and I were close growing up but as we grew into adulthood we went our own separate ways. We didn't stay in close contact. Eric and I were a little closer. Maurice went to college. Eric went to the army.

I moved one particular day after Eric returned home from the army and we were talking about our lives growing up in the home. Eric said, "Remember when we were little and people would tease me saying I am a mama's boy and I didn't want to do anything but stay home, and I would never stay overnight anywhere?" I said, "Yeah," then he shared that he didn't know when it would be the last time we would see our mom alive. I instantly cried; the tears wouldn't stop running. Emotions started rising as we remembered when my dad beat him so badly that his body was bruised and swollen and he was a totally different color. Eric and I were the only two there. I cried while he was being beaten. That beating destroyed Eric mentally but he still survived. Eric never looked at our dad the same. He left and didn't return home for years. When Eric returned home we celebrated, then he moved on and never returned again. He was found dead and that was one of the most hurtful things for my mom to lose one of her children.

I could remember talking to my mom and we were talking about how they were taught to stay in their marriage no matter what goes on. Back then a lot of women were being verbally abused and beaten; then they were told to take them to the bedroom. My question was for what? I remember one particular time my mom and dad were in their room and I heard my mom screaming, "Stop Eddie!" and I went to the bedroom door and tried to go in. It was locked so I fell on the floor crying. My mom did have the courage to leave but she was told to go back. I asked my mom why did you stay? She told me that we were too young for her to leave. My brothers and I took part in trying to help my mom. I picked up the iron to give to my mom to bash my dad in the head, then I grabbed him. He smacked me in the shoulder and I slid across the floor. My brother grabbed him so my mom could get away. My dad had my mom in the basement; I even saw my dad pull a knife up to my mom's throat in the basement. I sat on the steps crying. My brother, Maurice, got some size and stood up to our dad. Maurice got word from someone that our dad was beating our mom so he ran home. Now my mom's friend, Annette, told her if she kept going back one day he's going to kill her.

Economics

Gracie and Eddie both had very good jobs in the 70's. My mom worked at Auto Specialties. My dad worked at Clark Equipment. My brothers and I didn't have to want for nothing; our parents were very good providers. One day my dad was beating my mom and she got away and we went to my aunt's house. My dad's oldest sister saw my mom was bleeding in her face so my dad tried to grab my mom. His sister told him he was not going to hit on my mom in her house. Gracie left again.

This time Eddie had the whole house remodeled. I'm telling you we had a nice home. There were glass sliding doors, lazy Suzy cabinets, even a black range stove with smooth eyes, counter top, and black marble floors. He convinced my mom to come back home, so she went back home.

Things were good for a while. Now I know my mom attended church all the time because we had to be there. We were made to participate in the church as we were growing up. I remember being in a choir. We were at church sunshine band; we worked as junior ushers; then the junior choir; we were at the church all of the time. I remember the saints and all the children on the altar tarrying for the Holy Ghost. Some had it, some acted like they had it. We were tired.

The Accuser Of The Brethren

Eddie, my dad, started accusing my mom of cheating since we were gone all the time. Back then the church travelled a lot so dad convinced himself that my mom was cheating. He beat her so bad that it looked like the meat in her face was hanging out. That's when Gracie decided to leave for good. I was about 13 or 14 years old. Gracie called her best friend, and they made plans when they were going to get her out of there. The day my mom left was the day my dad worked overtime. She left my brothers there. About a week later here comes my brothers with their clothes in the trunk of the car. Their words were, " that man is crazy." Gracie never went back.

 As for my dad, his mind snapped meaning he lost his mind. My brothers and I tried to go and see him. He said Eric and I weren't his children. Eric attempted to go see him again. Eddie wouldn't let him in. He said he didn't know Eric. Eric said, "It's me daddy, your son Eric". My dad said, "I don't know no Eric." Eric said, "Well when my dad gets back, tell him his son Eric came by".

Growing up back then adults would say you don't tell what goes on in the household. I'm here to say if someone is being hurt, beaten, raped, touched inappropriately; tell. Parents please talk to your children; you could be saving someone's life.

52

"The words of king Lemuel, the
prophecy that his mother taught
him. What, my son? and what, the
son of my womb? and what, the son
of my vows?" Proverbs 31:1-2.

God Said Not So

All the years of my life I only knew about holiness. As I grew into an adult the world seemed to be fun and exciting so I decided to go into the world. I did the same things that some other people would do. I had children. I sold drugs. I fought. I carried weapons. I was having fun. But God spared my life. He had and he still has a plan for my life. Somebody was praying for me. Today I can thank you Lord for my salvation. God didn't expose me in my mess.

Today I have a hard time breathing because of my lungs. My breathing was affected. I have to have an oxygen tank. Also, my throat is sore. I continue to throw up phlegm. I panic because it's hard to breathe. I get tired walking from one room to the other.

I yet have the victory. I am taking care of four grand kids. Rayquon has lived with me since he was little. He is now 15 years old. He went home but he came back when he was a second grader. Rayquon was born autistic. He used to tap on things a lot. Noise bothers him.

In spite of that Rayquon always makes sure I have my medicine. He's a good little male nurse. He lies next to me when I get sick. He's the one who calls 911.

Marriage was not good. I was married three times, twice to the same man. Then lupus developed. My husband's name is Ronald Wooden. This illness was very new to him. In the beginning, he was afraid and didn't know how to react to it. Now that years have gone by he stands tall and makes sure I get to my appointments and get what I need.

I have defied the doctors and lived to be the ripe old age of fifty-two at present. I have been President of the YWCC for several years, and Hospitality secretary in my local church. I cook, clean, knit, I sew. Cooking is my specialty   I function as a wife, mother, grandmother, and daughter. God has blessed me tremendously.

"But ye are a chosen generation, a royal priesthood, an holy nation, a peculiar people; that ye should shew forth the praises of him who hath called you out of darkness into his marvelous light." I Peter 2:9

Praise the Lord!

In this book I talked about my experiences in the hospital and how God delivered me from sickness and from death. During the last encounter in the hospital I fell into a deep depression. I felt so alone. The enemy had taken over. I was so angry. One night I thought about crying, I guess I was feeling so much guilt thinking about Rayquan, my grandson, and wondering who was going to get him. Rayquan needed me and I needed him. I cried because he has been with me most of his life. I decided to make a phone call to a prayer warrior named Lyneva Dalton who is also my aunt. Lyneva went into a spiritual prayer language and after I hung up the phone I started feeling so much guilt. I started repenting about everything I could think of from the time I was little to adulthood, so much build up in me that I hadn't repented about. You know what? It felt so good to pour my heart out to the Lord. Then I heard the Spirit of the Lord say "I've been waiting on you", meaning He had been waiting on a true repentance. When I heard that I cried even harder to know the Lord truly loves me and to know the Lord heard a true repentance. What a great feeling it is.

Now I praise the Lord for everything. I praise Him when I can't breathe very well; I let nothing stop my praise. I praise God for my good and I praise Him when things are bad. I praise Him in a hymn and a song. I praise Him with a clap of my hands and when it gets real good I praise Him with a stomp of my feet, then start stepping on the devil's head which drives him crazy. I love praising God. I praise Him knowing He's going to deliver my girls. I praise Him when I'm going through. I praise Him when the girls are going through. I know because they call, and I tell them God has His Hands on them! The Lord is so good He even alarms me when they are in trouble. I pray. I praise Him all the time because He gives me new grace and mercy every day that I awake.

There is no greater love than that. There is nothing in this world worthy of praise but only when you are praising our Lord and Savior Jesus Christ and our Father for sending Him. I even praise the Holy Spirit for keeping us. If I knew then what I know now about serving the Lord I would have given my life to Him a long time ago. I hope and pray that this book will motivate you to be encouraged in the Lord. Jesus is the best thing that ever happened to me. He keeps me humble; He keeps me from getting angry when I deserve to be.

In my closing of this book, I thank you for allowing me to give my testimony. Most of all, I praise God for allowing me to write this book. To God be His glory because without Him this would be nothing.

59

"Withhold not correction from child:
for if thou beatest him with the rod,
he shall not die. Thou shalt beat
him with the rod, and shalt deliver
his soul from hell. My son, if thine
heart be wise, my heart shall
rejoice, even mine." Proverbs 23: 13,
14, 15.

An Answer to a Mother`s Cry

In a home where there was sicknesses and various dysfunctions I was being called to Christ. It makes you improve one's mind to fight for life. As I acknowledged the call, God showed me how to improve the right fight in life, to become strong willed to fight the right fight.

In the meantime I was praying for others - praying for my grand children and children, praying for family, all my loved ones, and people God enabled me to pray for the rest of my appointed time. There's nothing like a Mother's cry. We can't avoid when GOD calls us. Not for fear, or sitting getting sore, being lazy, up to nothing. We have to get up and face it, answer the call. We have to come face to face with reality to move the kingdom of God. There is a cry out from the Lord who carried the cross for our burdens. The reason? For his grace, we know, next Jesus carries me. When I had no strength to live, God then carried me. Crying, I let him.

There's nothing like a mother's cry to remind me that I must keep going. There's nothing like a mother's cry to remind me that I am worthy. Crying Abba, Father, Holy, Holy, Holy One. How holy is His name for He is my life. For the weak He made strong. He called me. He heard my cry, enabling me to answer the call to become what he wants me to be. I pray this even now. I have to fight so I cry to God thanking him for hearing me!

I give thanks to God for hearing my mother's cry for me to be healed.

Conclusion

If it had not been for the Lord on my side, tell me where would I be. I'll tell you where I'd be. I wouldn't be here to tell this story. The Lord has been mighty, mighty good to me. Not only is He a healer but He's a Savior.

On January 13, 1999 God saved my soul. Back in 1998 Elder Kerwin Hudson brought me to the front of the church. The Holy Spirit knocked me out. I couldn't move. Pastor Wells III kept me for last. He prayed that I would get no rest in my spirit until I surrendered to God. I felt that I was missing something. I broke up with my boyfriend. I decided I wanted to be saved.

My mother doesn't think she whipped me much. I say yes you did. My mother said only when I needed it. We laugh about it.

I want to thank all the people who helped me to put together the things I couldn't remember. God bless you all. I also would like to thank Mother Greta Joseph for her valuable time.

A Prayer For Your Will For This Book
God Said Not So!

Father, for all that come in possession of this book let your spirit fill these pages. Father God, I am praying that this would persuasively bring your people everywhere to you! Father God, I leave my generation my prayer legacy for all. When asking God to forgive you, you say, God have mercy on me. When praying for help, wisdom and joy, in your life, just to serve God you said Lord, I am asking for your grace in this life for myself and others.

Lord let this book be a small praise. Lord give a word to the hearts of the readers that they may lean and depend on you Lord, to come when they stumble or fall, for we have many inconsistencies. Father we send this prayer first to my children - Kesha and Dameka, and to my grandchildren - Rayquan, Travon, Nyesha and Darrell thanking GOD for having seen numerous miracles. God has worked, even showing how God even presented my father and my brothers in life a chance to come to him. God I'm praying that my girls and grands don't fight the Word, but put up a fight in a path of righteousness so that you Lord God will send the angels to show them YOU! Even my family, friends, loved ones, and the readers of this book, Lord, destroy every evil path th will try to tempt them. I bind that now! Let your loving power, Lord, on all shine! Save loved ones and who ever comes to read this book. Oh Lord bless this book for your glory.

I am praying that the people see that you brought me from a coma, that you said NO! I pray they see your miracle in me.

Coming from a coma! But God said NO! Not so. God I am praying that You Lord save the seeds of the ones you have called! Healed! Use them as you will and set them free letting them know that nothing can hold down your called servants!

I pray now! The words you gave in this book will bring to pass the will for people to wait on the Lord! Wait for the Lord God's healing! Wait on the Lord God's miracles! Wait on His strength! Wait on Him to work it all out!

Photos

66

Me and my mom

It's Me

My daughter, Kesha

My daughter, Dameka

My grandson Rayquan

Dameka

Me and my two daughters

My husband, Ronald Wooden

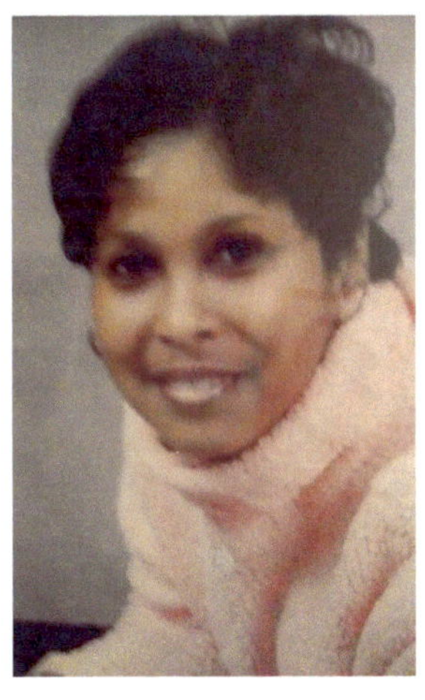

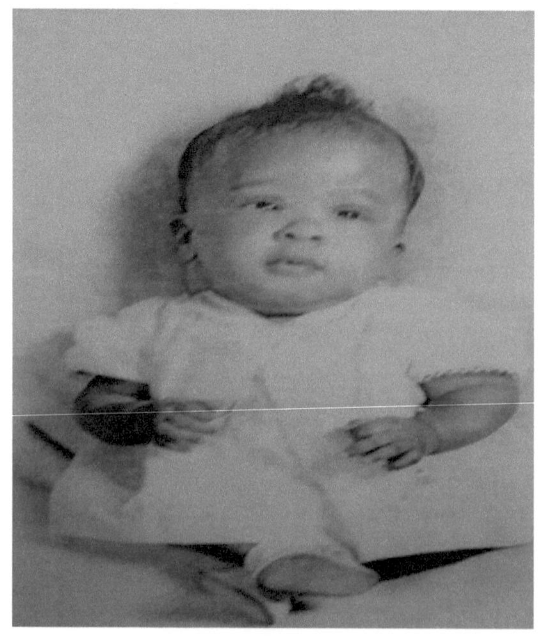

The miracle baby

My Children and My Grands

My daughter

My grandson Rayquon

About the Author
Tamara Bowman Wooden

Tamara M. Wooden, 52, of Benton Harbor went home to be with the Lord Wednesday March 8, 2017. The home going celebration was held Saturday, March 18, 2017 at the Greater Community Christian Fellowship COGIC, Benton Harbor.

Tammy, as she was fondly known, was born June 5, 1964. She was the daughter of Eddie Bowman (deceased) and Gracie Yarbrough Holliday. Tammy was a 1984 Benton Harbor High School graduate. She enjoyed life and loved the Lord. She was an active member of Greater Community Christian Fellowship COGIC.

Tammy worked for Atlantic Automotive for years. She loved cooking, writing, and loved people, especially babies.

Tammy gave birth to two beautiful daughters, despite the doctors giving Tammy up to age 10 to live. God said live on my child. I have more work for you to do. She was united in Holy Matrimony to Ronald Wooden, August 25, 2002.

Tammy leaves to cherish her memories and carry on her legacy: her husband, Ronald, her loving mother, Gracie Holliday, daughters Kesha and Dameka, brother, Maurice, sister Linda, brothers, Darrell and Roderick Holliday and four grandchildren, Rayquan, Travon, Nyesha and Darrell.

Words From the Editor

Greta Elaine Joseph

It is with great pleasure that I present this autobiography written by Tammy Bowman Wooden and many witnesses. Sister Tammy was such a joy to work with. She knew what she wanted and she asked me to help her produce it. We spent many evenings at her apartment as she reminisced and wrote of the goodness of God. She was such a sweet and delightful soul. She was always trying to make everyone happy and showed such concern for others. As we sat and went over her writings she was very particular about what she wanted and how she wanted it.

Tammy loved the Lord and she wanted every word to honor him. She knew she was a walking miracle and she wanted to convey that in her book. Whenever she didn't remember she would call up a witness and send me to interview them. She knew there were many times in her life when she was not aware of what was going on as she lay in the hospital bed BUT GOD SAID NOT SO! The devil did not take her life. She lived out her purpose and was able to approve her book before going home to the Father.

Although Tammy was able to see her published work, it was a serious battle to finally get it into your hands. The computer kept malfunctioning, work was often lost or erased. I had to eventually travel all the way across the country as I continued in spiritual warfare. Angels were battling in heavenly places to release this book. BUT GOD SAID NOT SO!

I only pray that she is praising God as you, the readers, experience the power of God that filled her life and sustained her for 52 years. Sleep on, angel of God. We will meet again.

Tamara Marie